FOOTSTEPS

THE Inuit

Ruth Thomson

Contents

WATTS BOOKS
London • New York • Sydney

Who are the Inuit?

Inuit people live in the Arctic, one of the coldest places in the world. There are no trees, tall buildings or railways and very few roads. They rely on rivers and the sea for transport.

The ground is frozen for much of the year, so people cannot grow crops.

The Inuit live on the coasts of Canada, Alaska and Greenland. In the past, they survived by fishing and by hunting seal and caribou. The animals provided them with food, fur for clothes, skins for tents, tools and fuel.

Today, the Inuit live in houses. They can buy everything they need from shops.

A scrimshaw picture

Visiting whalers taught the Inuit to carve
pictures on the ivory tusks of walrus.
These are called scrimshaw pictures.

You will need:

Black wax crayon   Scissors   Card

Follow the steps . . .

1. Cut a piece of card
   in the shape of a tusk.

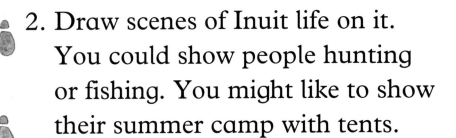

2. Draw scenes of Inuit life on it.
   You could show people hunting
   or fishing. You might like to show
   their summer camp with tents.

Hunting

In the past, the Inuit moved from place to place, hunting animals on foot.

In spring and summer they hunted seal and walrus from boats called kayaks. They speared them with harpoons and killed only what they needed. All year round they fished in lakes and streams.

Now the Inuit can buy food and clothes in shops. They work during the week. Many Inuit still hunt and fish for their own food at weekends. They are keeping alive the skills of the past and teaching them to their children.

Many Inuit travel by snowmobile or motor boat and hunt with rifles. Others prefer to use sleds and traditional weapons.

A sled

You will need:

Balsa wood   Stiff card   Fabric scraps

Scissors   Paint and brush   String

Polystyrene chips   Sandpaper   Glue

Follow the steps . . .

1. Ask an adult to cut two strips of balsa wood, 25cm by 2cm, for the runners. Sandpaper one edge to make it curved, like this.

2. Cut and paint several strips of card, 6cm long and 2cm wide. Glue them along the runners.

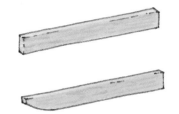

3. Glue some rolled-up fabric scraps on to the sled. Add some snow blocks made of polystyrene.

4. Glue a length of string to both runners.

An Arctic frieze

The Inuit respected the animals they hunted and decorated their weapons with pictures of them.

You will need:

White paper   Paint and brush   Scissors
Pencil   Glue

Follow the steps . . .

1. Sketch the background for your frieze in pencil and paint it.

2. Paint and cut out some Arctic animals and birds.

3. Glue them on to the background.

4. You could add an Inuit as well.

Clothes

The Inuit need to wear warm clothes for ten months of the year.

The women still make many clothes from animal skins. It takes time to prepare the skins. The women chew them to make them soft. Then they sew the clothes with tight stitches to make them waterproof.

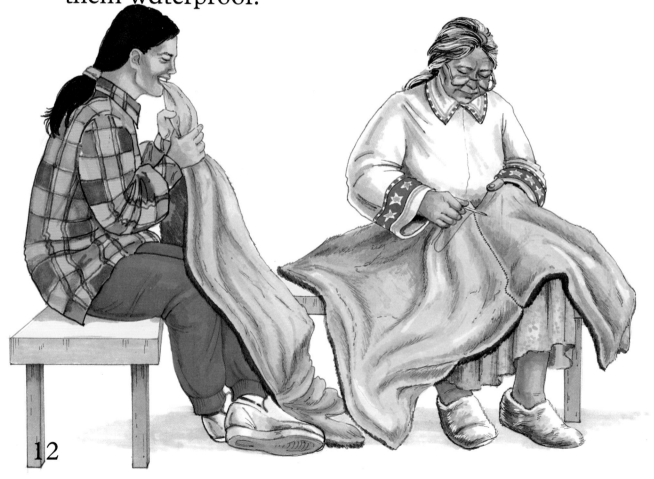

Trousers and hooded coats, called parkas,
are made from caribou and polar bear skin.
Mittens and boots are made of seal skin.
Under these outer clothes, the Inuit wear
another layer of soft fur clothes as well.

Many Inuit wear modern clothes at home.
They still wear fur clothes when they
go hunting.

Mittens

Needle and thread   Pencil   Card   Scissors

Felt   Ribbon   Pins   Cotton wool

Follow the steps . . .

1. Draw around your hand on to some card, like this. Draw a line 20cm outside your hand shape. Cut along this outer line.

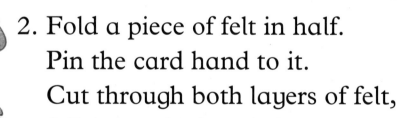

2. Fold a piece of felt in half. Pin the card hand to it. Cut through both layers of felt, following the hand shape. Turn the hand over and do the same thing again.

3. Sew each pair of felt pieces together. Turn them inside out. Sew cotton wool around the wrists.

Inuit collage

You will need:

White card   Brown paper   Black felt
Cotton wool   Fabric scraps   Glue
Felt-tip pens   String

Follow the steps . . .

1. Draw an Inuit figure on some
   white card. Give him or her
   a face and black felt hair.

2. Cut out a brown paper parka,
   fabric trousers, boots and mittens.
   Glue them on to your figure.

3. Add cotton wool
   and string trimmings.

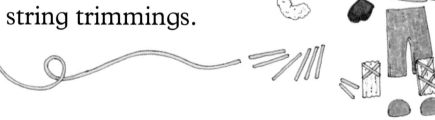

Homes

The Inuit live in settlements with shops, schools, churches and sports centres.

Their wooden houses are brought by sea, already partly made. The houses have central heating and triple glazing to keep them warm. They are built on stilts, so that heat from inside does not melt the frozen ground beneath.

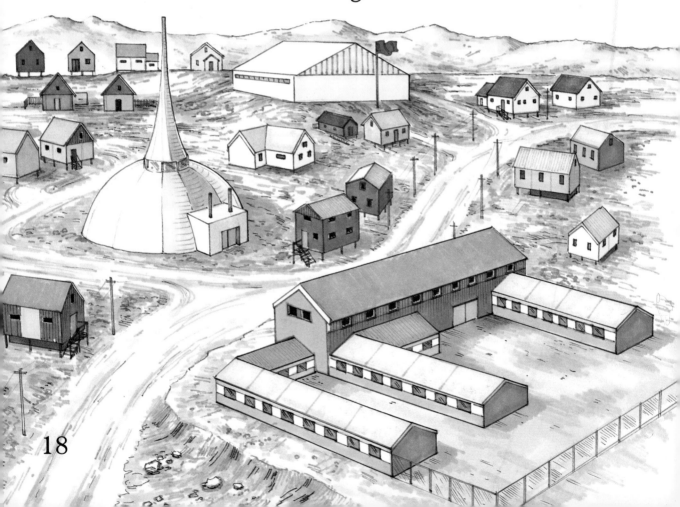

In the past, the Inuit lived in sod houses with roofs of turf over beams of whalebone.

During the winter hunting trips they built snowhouses. These were heated with seal-oil lamps and had a sleeping platform of snow. A tunnel entrance kept the cold wind out. In summer, they lived in tents made of skins.

Snowhouse

You will need:

Balloon   Bowl of water   Newspaper
PVA glue   Scissors   Card
White paint   Paintbrush   Salt

Follow the steps . . .

1. Cover half a blown-up balloon with newspaper strips, dipped in a glue and water mixture. Leave it to dry.

2. Pop the balloon and remove it. Trim the dome so that it sits flat. Cut a doorway in the dome. Snip along its edges.

3. Cut a card shape like this, with the flat edge about 15cm long. Bend and glue it to the doorway.

4. Paint the snowhouse white. While it is wet, sprinkle on salt to make it glisten.

Games

On dark winter days, when bad weather kept them inside, the Inuit used to play home-made games.

You will need:

Self-hardening or oven-baked clay   Modelling tools

Follow the steps . . .

1. Model some small Arctic animals and people from clay. Make sure each one has a wide, flat base. Let them dry.

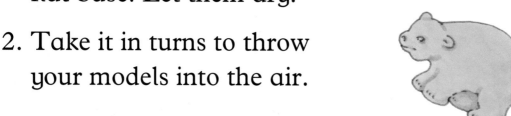

2. Take it in turns to throw your models into the air.

3. Gain five points each time one of your pieces lands upright, and one point if it lands on its side. The winner is the first player to reach thirty points.

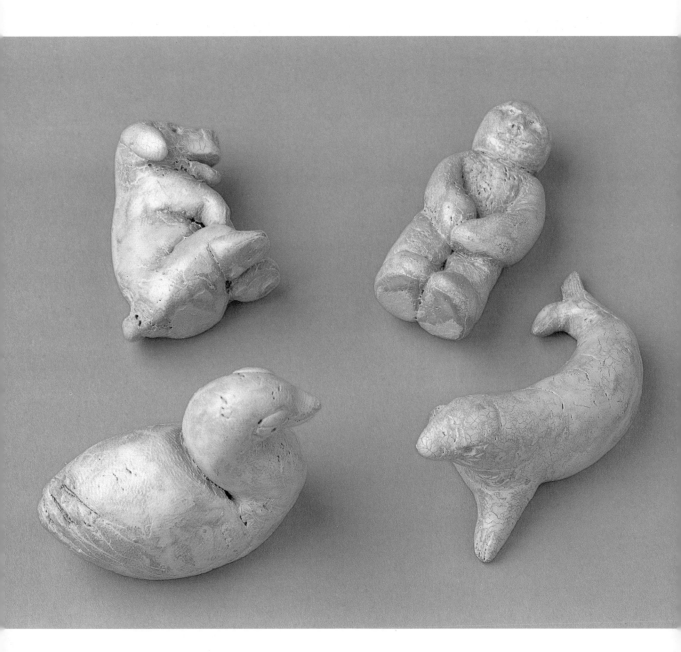

INDEX

Entries in *italics* are activity pages.

© 1996 Watts Books

Watts Books
96 Leonard Street
London EC2A 4RH

Franklin Watts Australia
14 Mars Road
Lane Cove
NSW 2066

UK ISBN 0 7496 2019 6

10 9 8 7 6 5 4 3 2 1

Editor: Annabel Martin
Consultant: Keith Lye
Design: Mike Davis
Artwork: Cilla Eurich
          Ruth Levy
Photographs: Peter Millard

A CIP catalogue record for this book is available from the British Library.

Dewey Decimal
Classification: 932

Printed in Malaysia